Catholic ABC

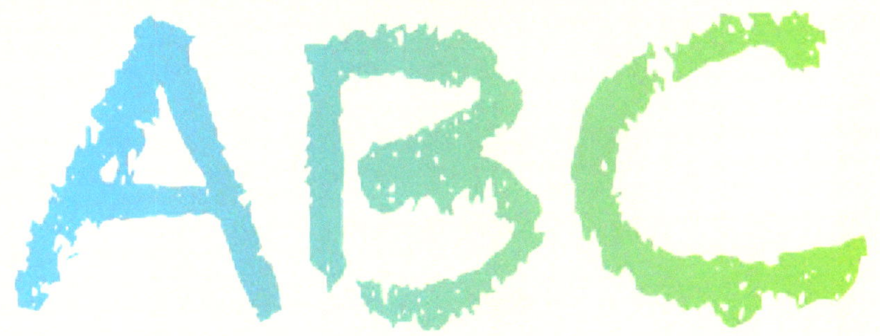

Hồng Phước Nguyễn

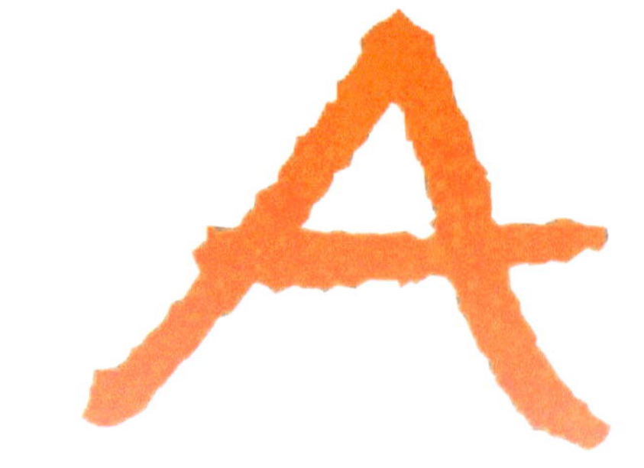

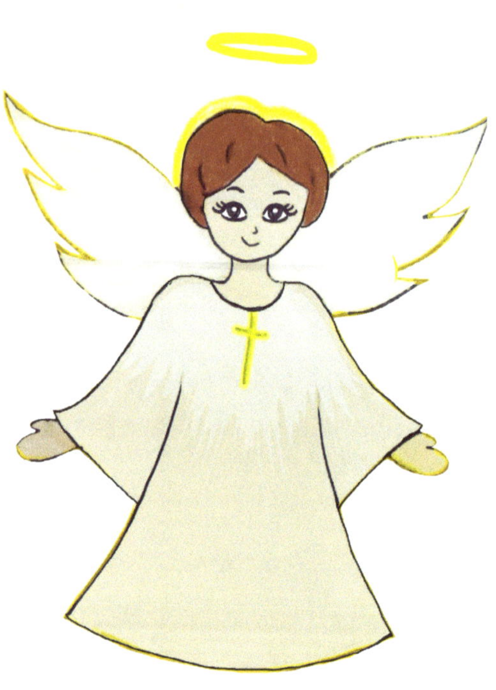

Angel

B

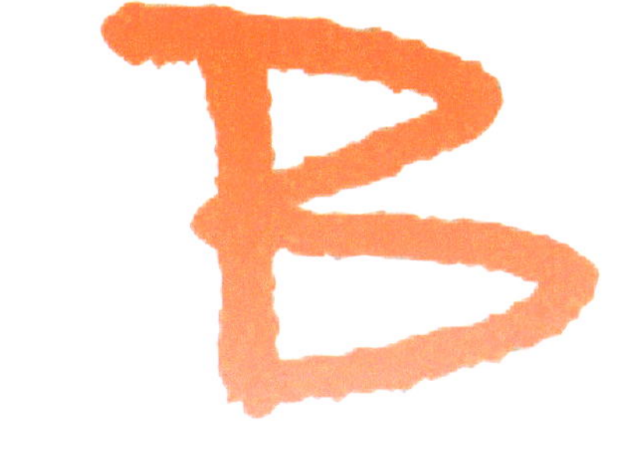

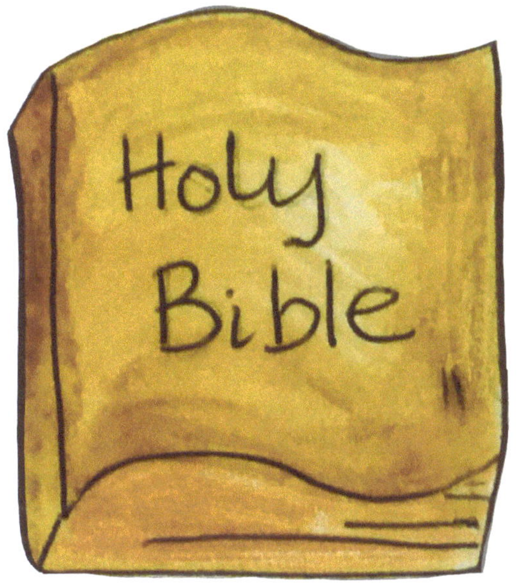

Bible

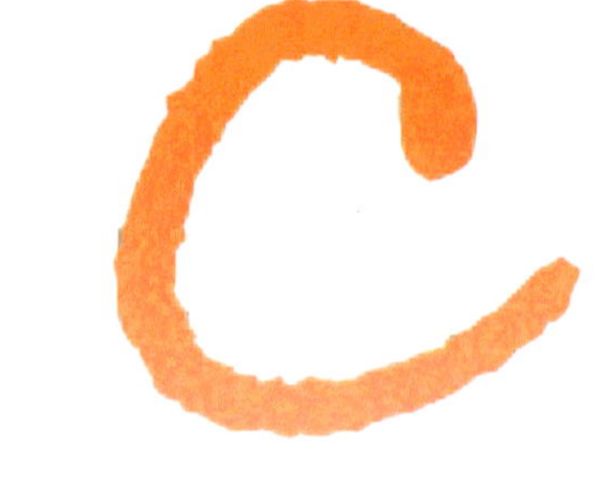

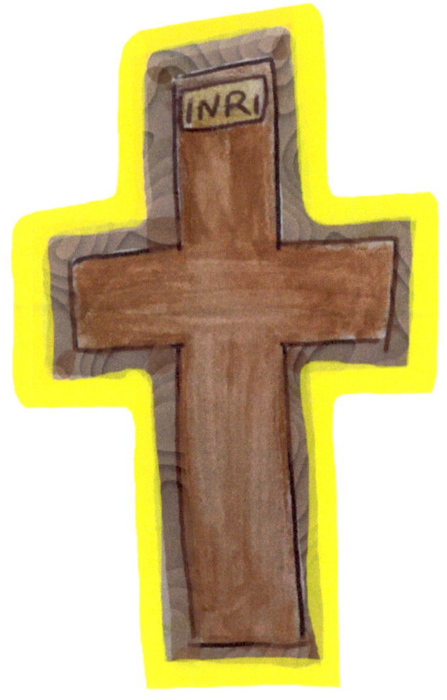

Cross

D

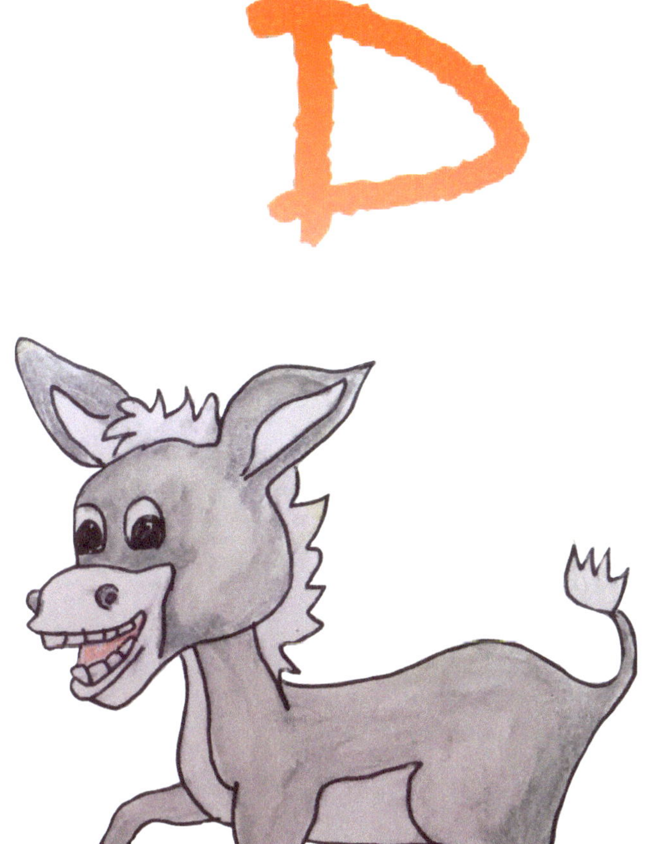

Donkey

E

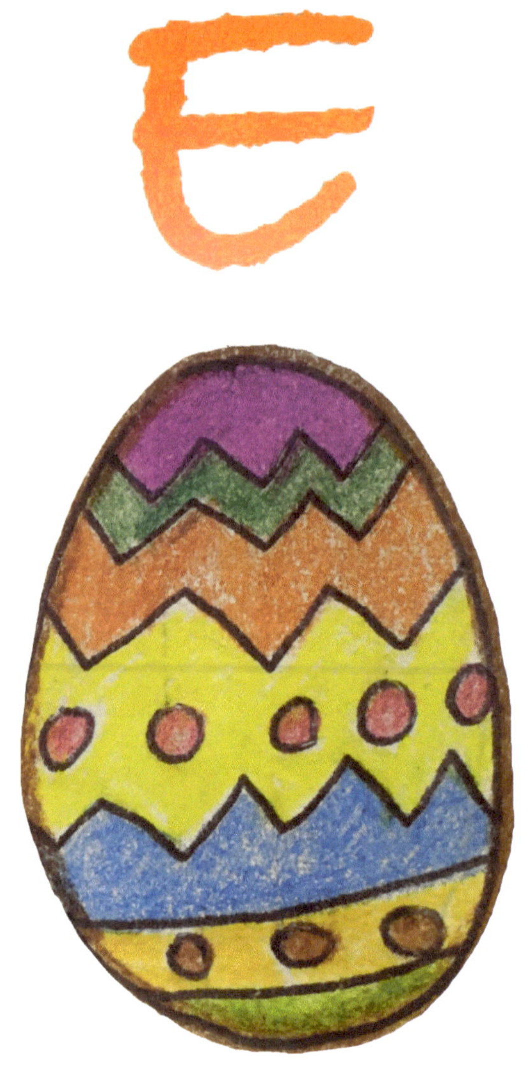

Easter

F

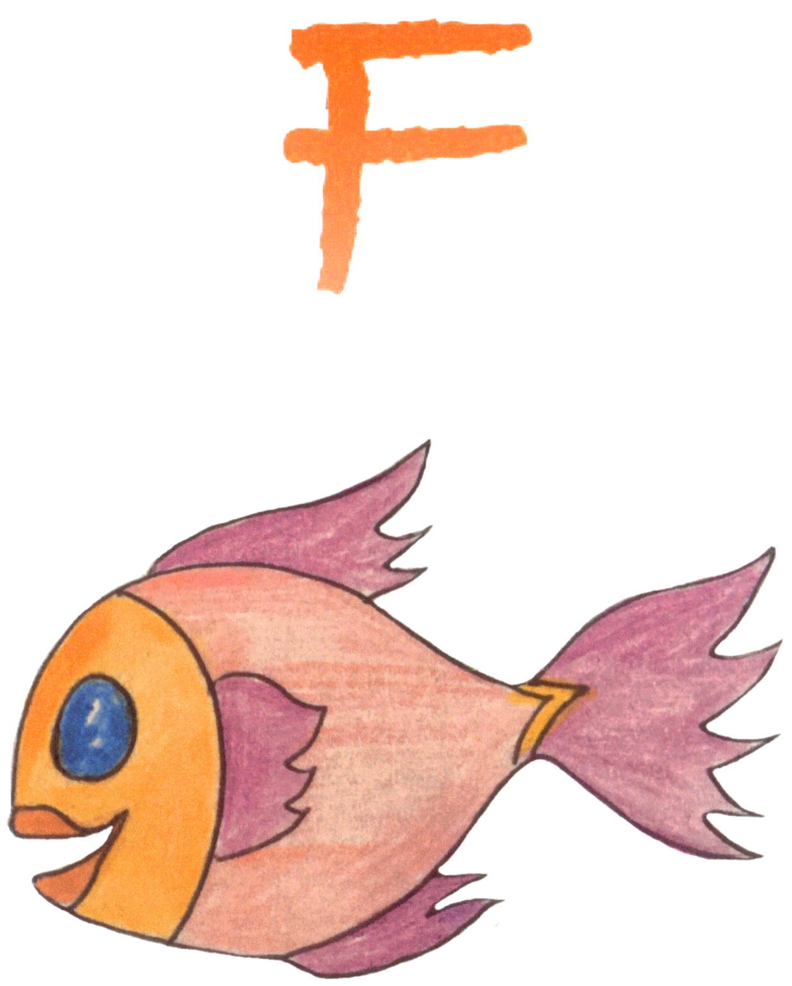

Fish

G

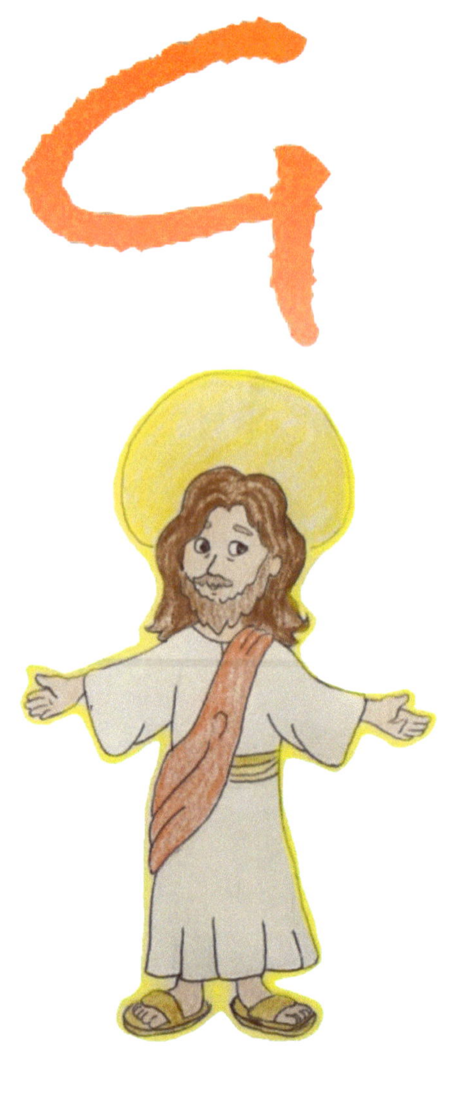

God

H

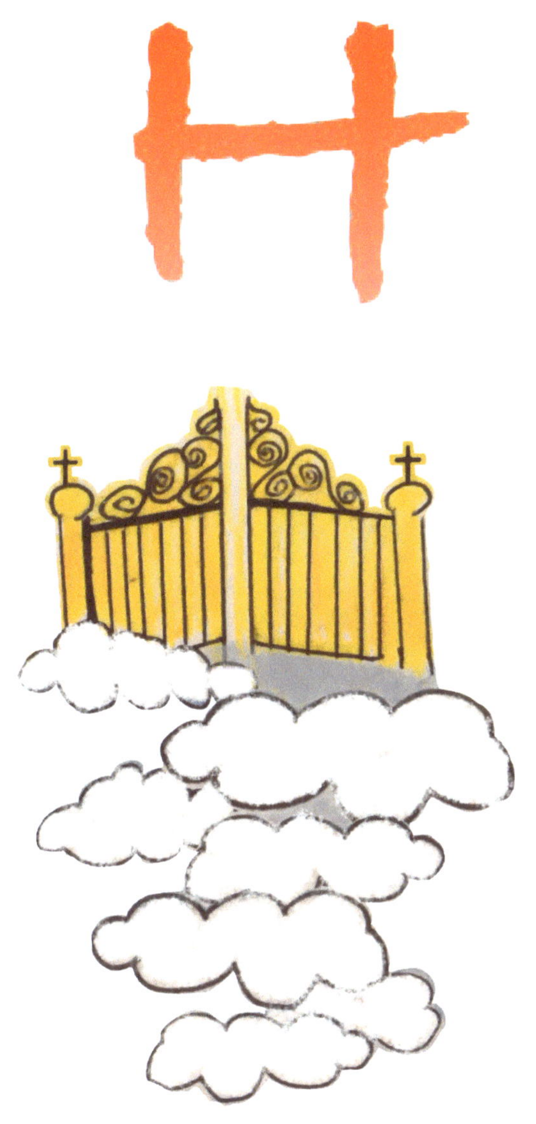

Heaven

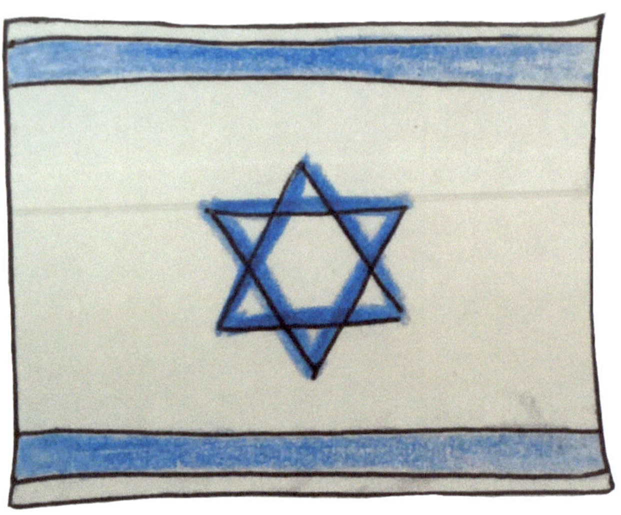

Israel

J

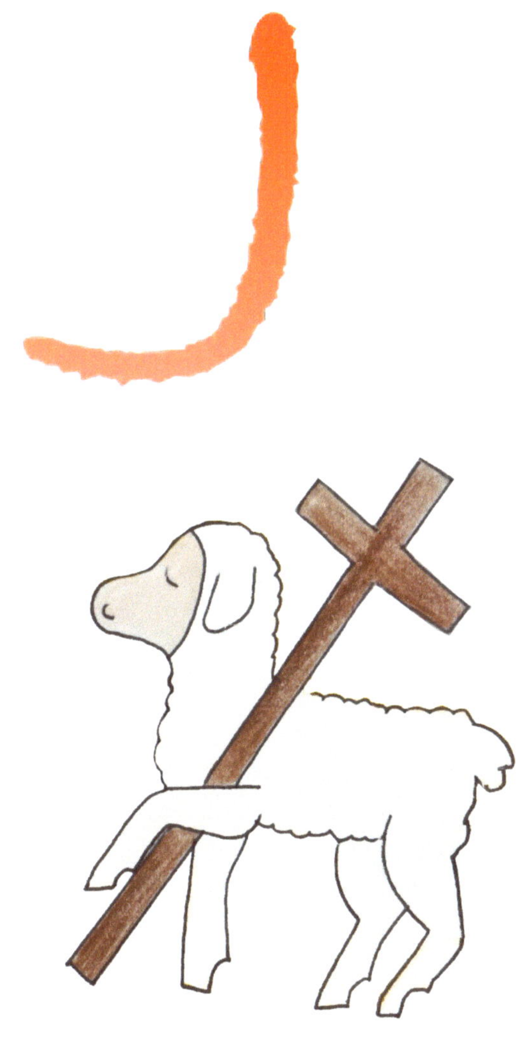

Jesus

K

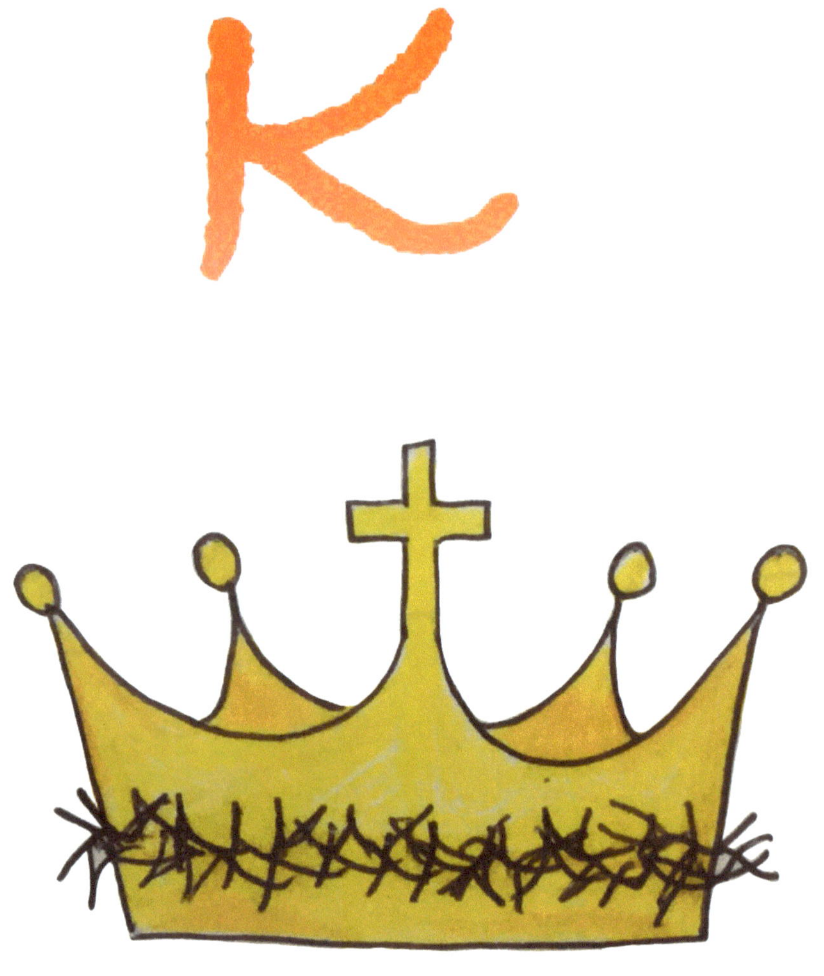

King

L

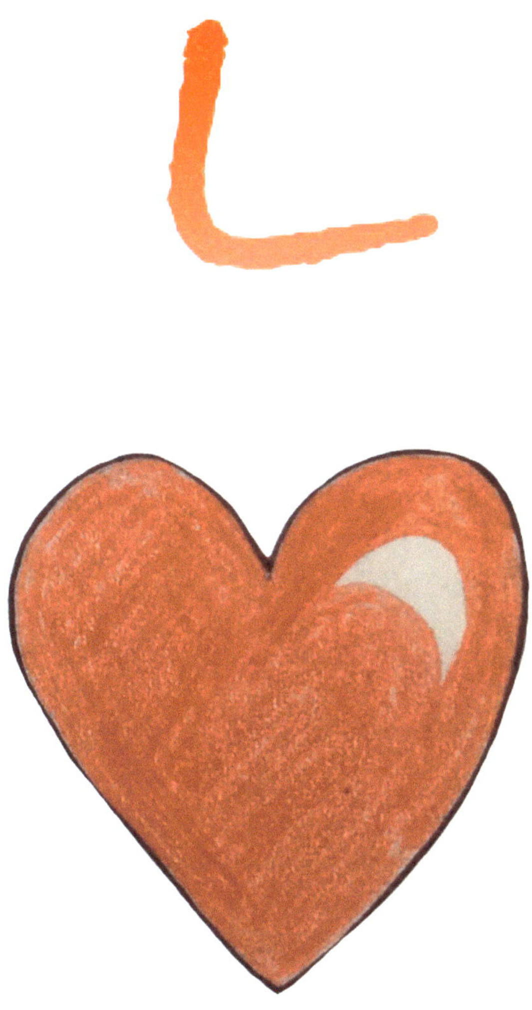

Love

M

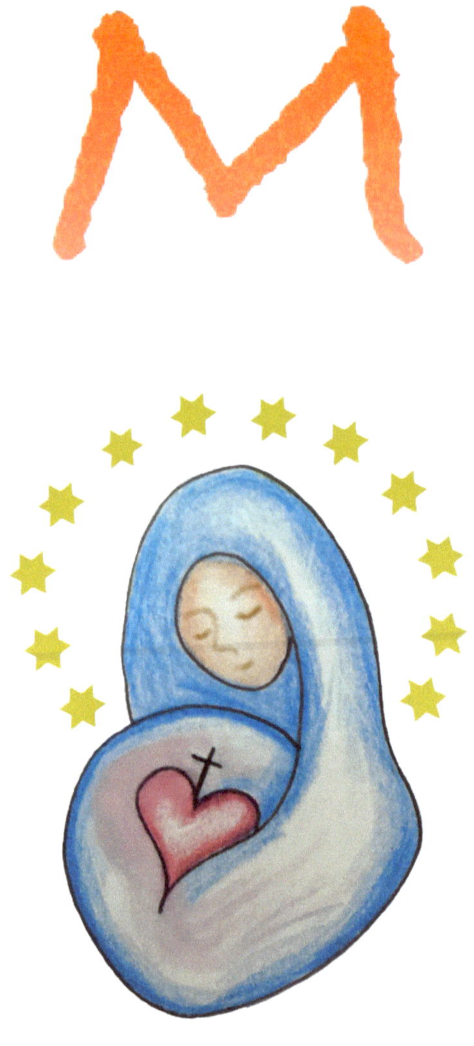

Mary

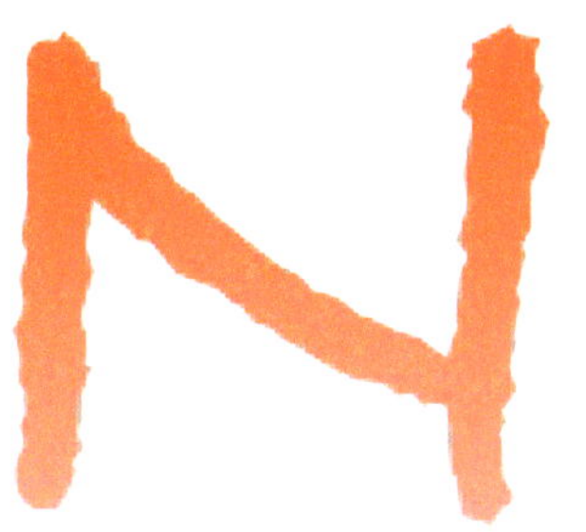

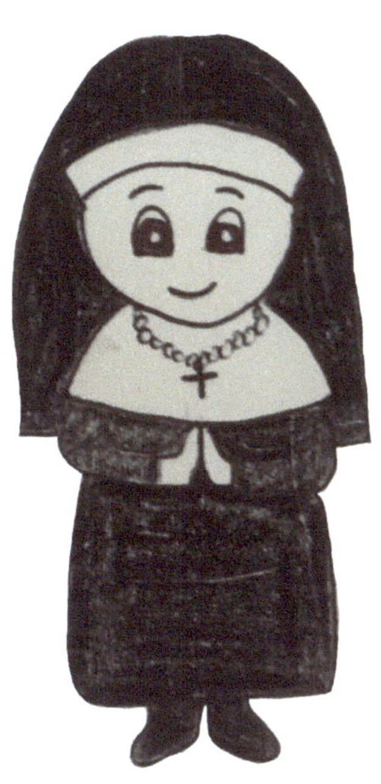

Nun

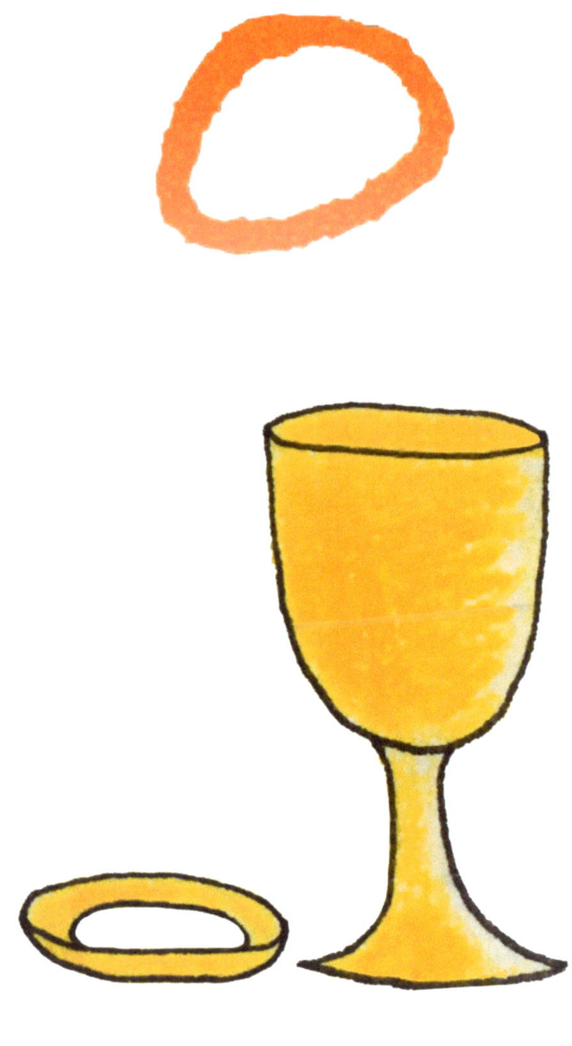

One

P

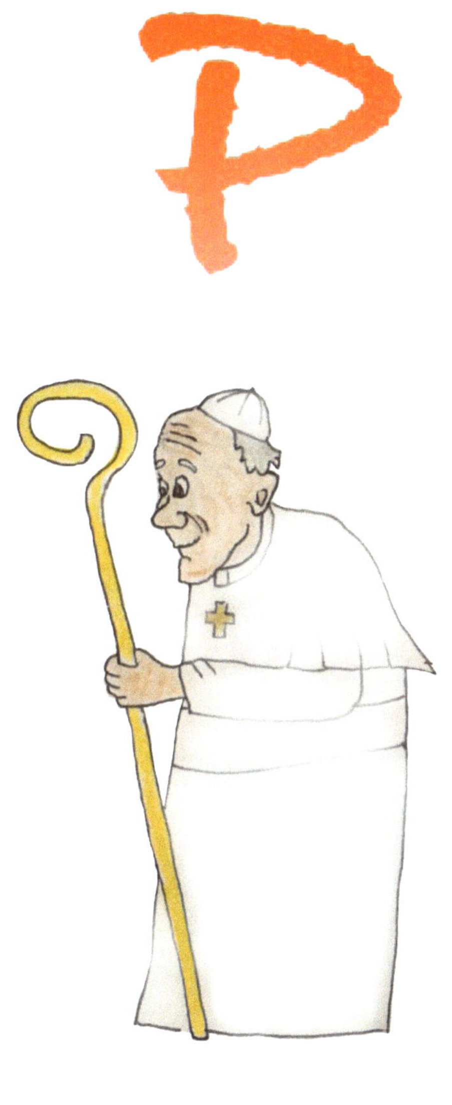

Pope

Q

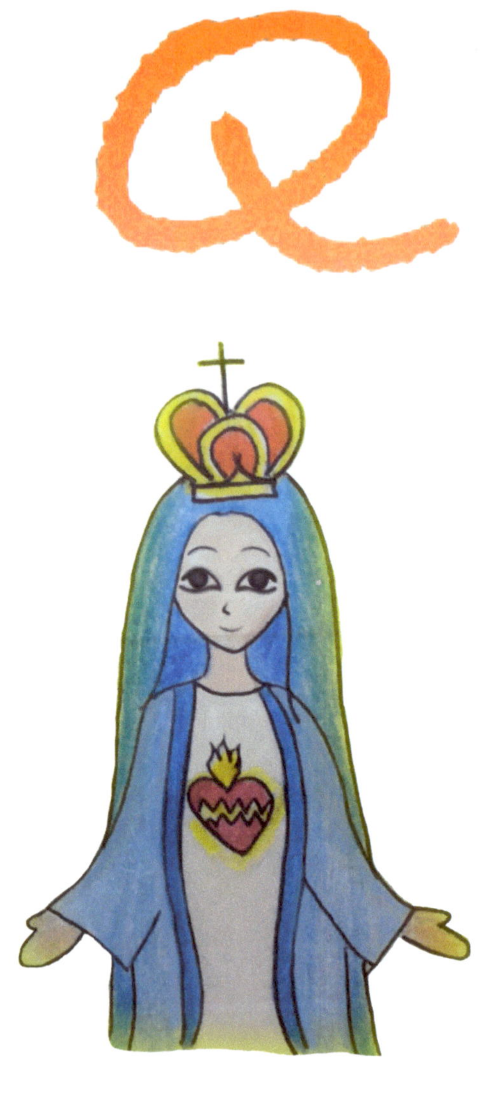

Queen

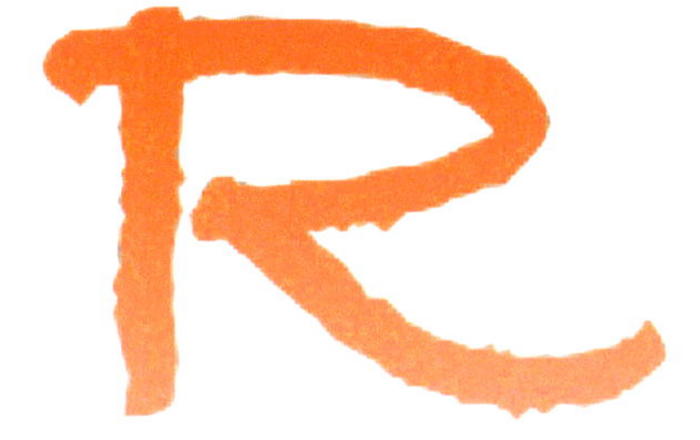

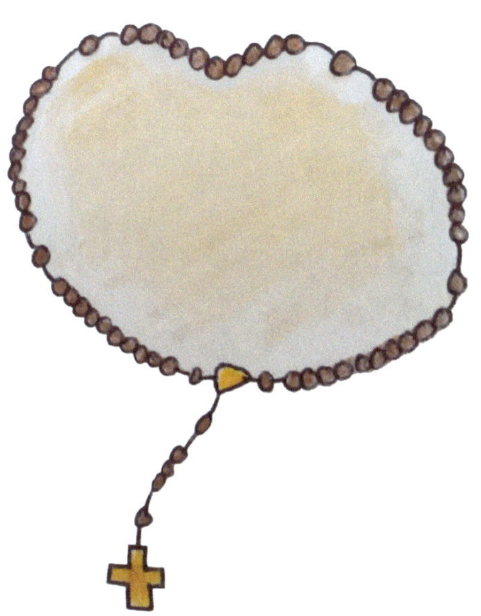

Rosary

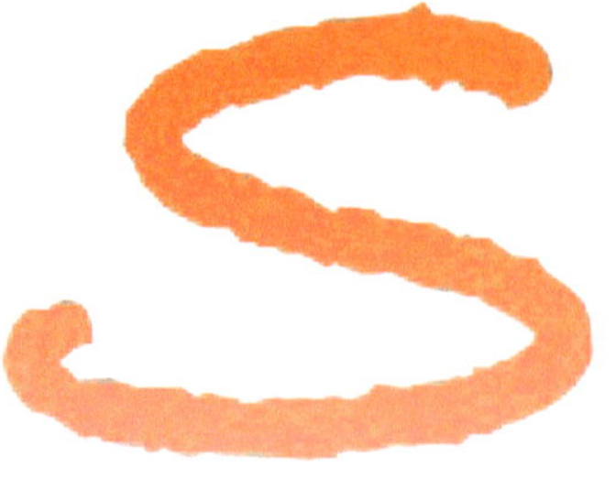

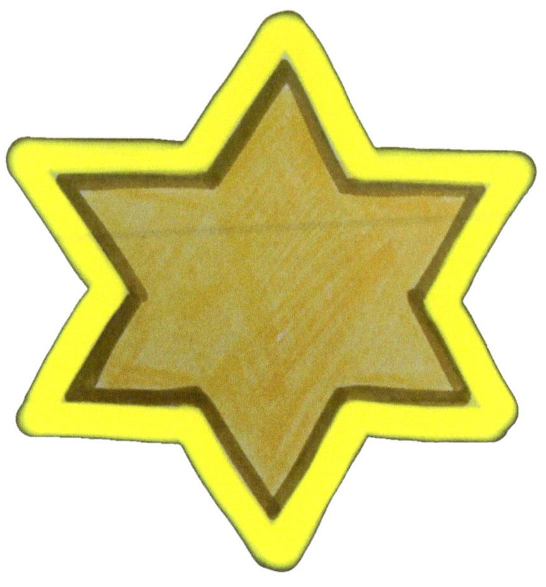

star

T

Trinity

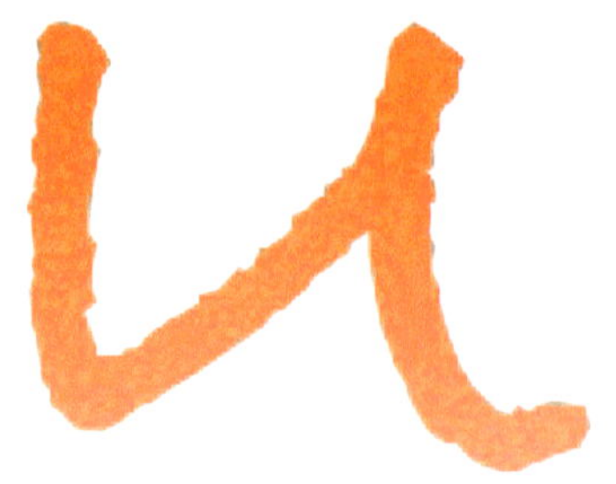

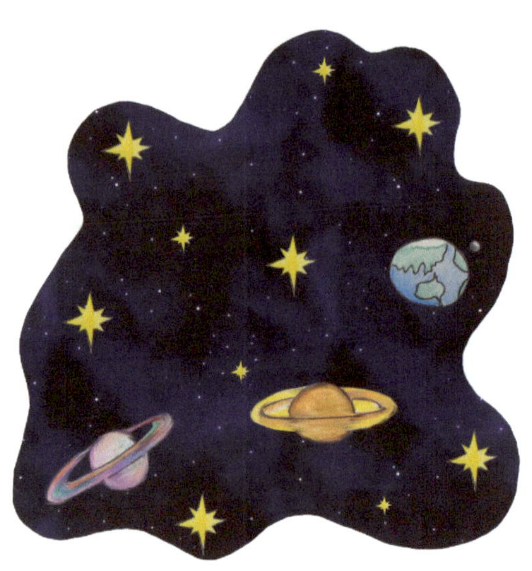

universe

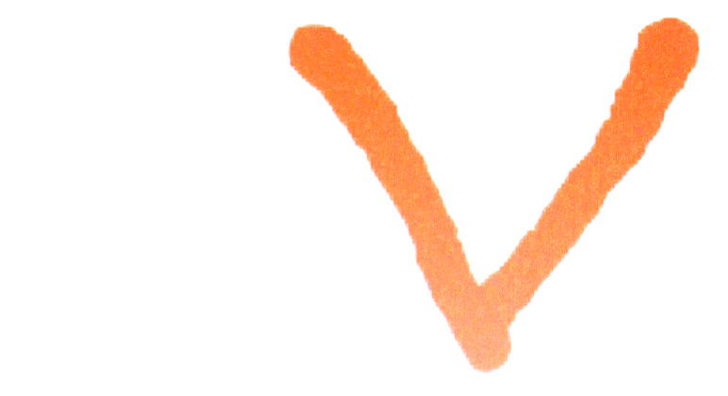

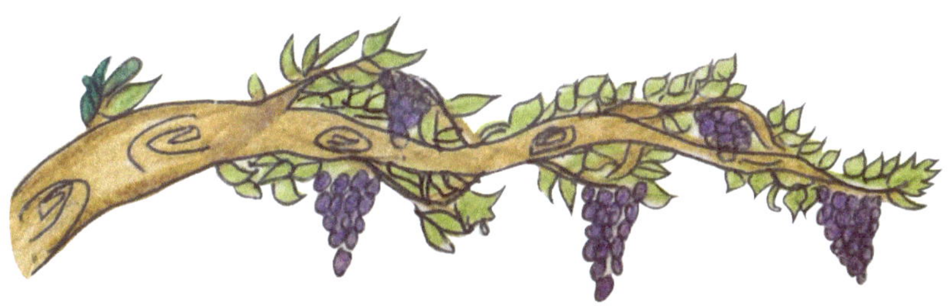

vine

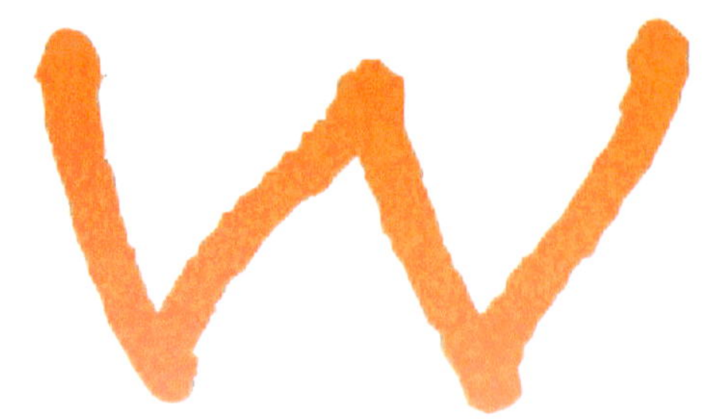

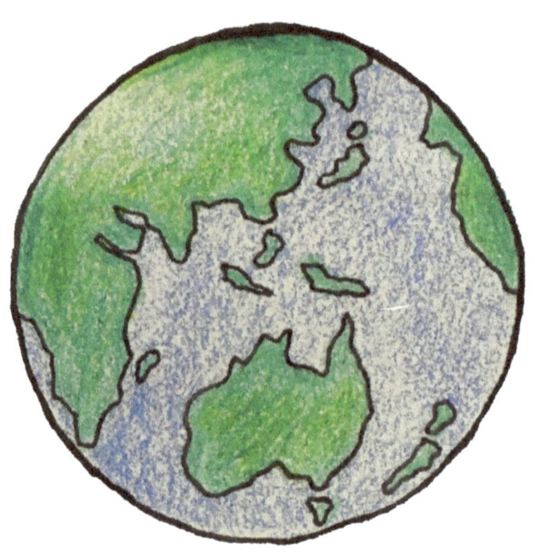

World

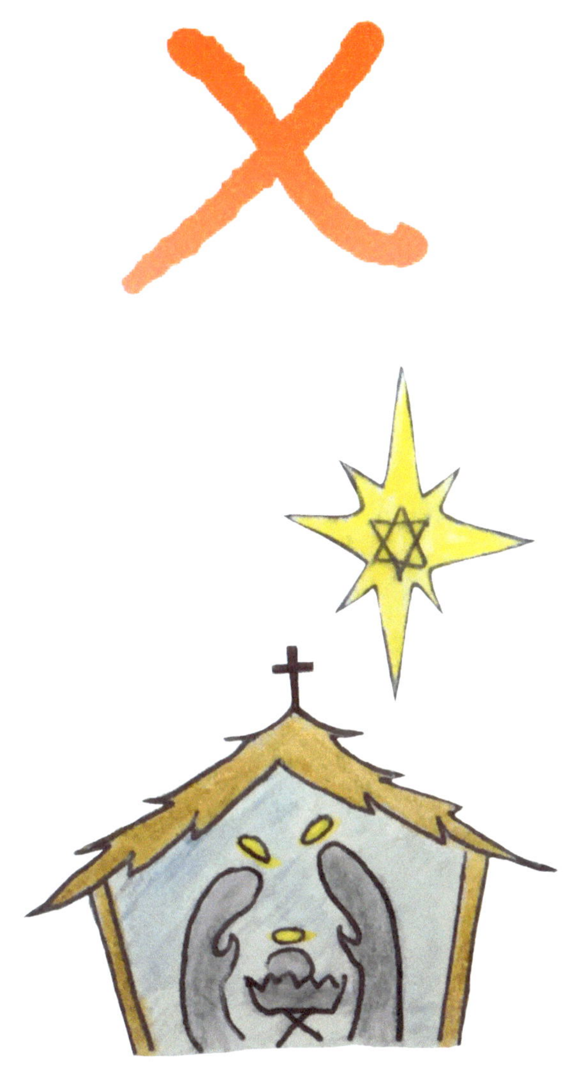

Xmas

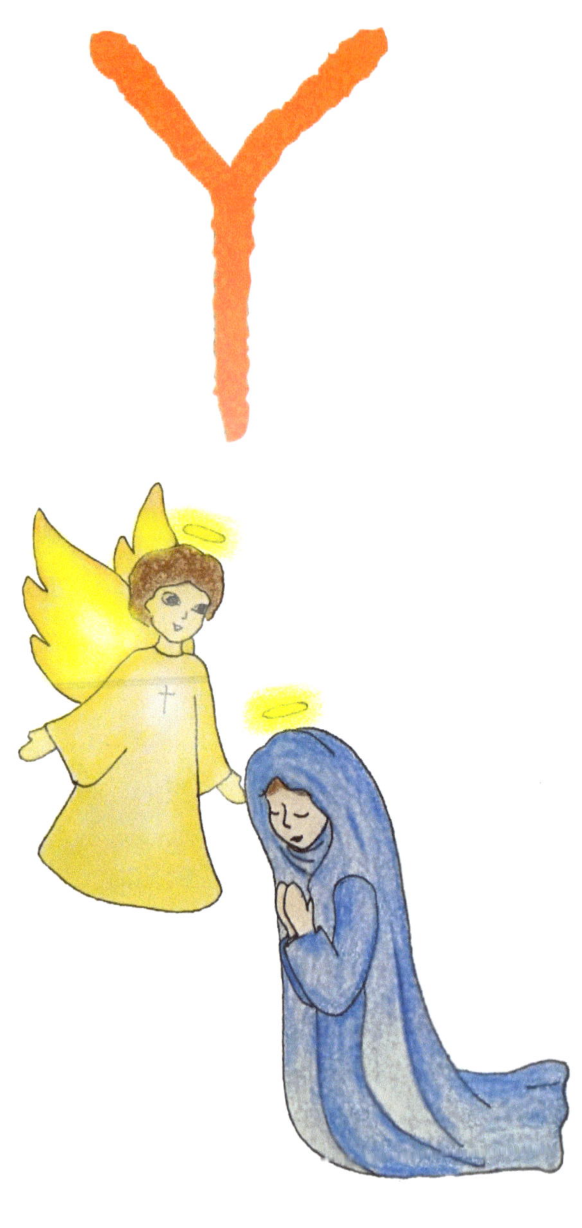

Yes

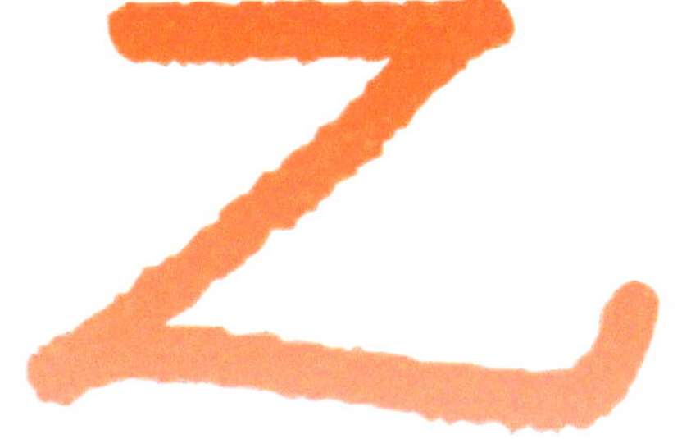

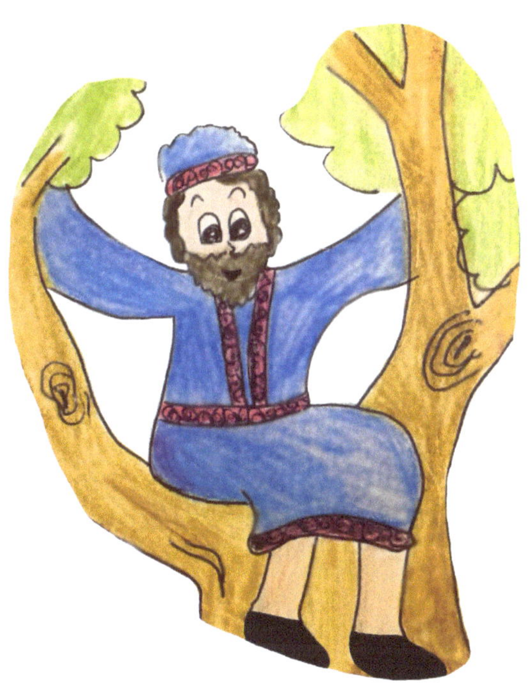

Zaccheus